6 Chords *for* Christmas

This book allows even the beginning guitarist to play and enjoy the magic of Christmas music.
By learning 6 simple chords for each song you will soon master 24 best-loved Christmas songs
and carols. This book doesn't use musical notation. All you need is to learn the chords
and their symbols. The chord boxes are printed at the beginning of each song to remind you, and the
chord changes are shown above the lyrics. If you find the pitch of a song outside your vocal range,
simply place your capo behind a suitable fret and use the same chord shapes.
The strum rhythm or picking pattern most suited to the song is left for you to decide.
This book guarantees hours of enjoyment for guitarists of all levels, as well as providing
a fine basis for building a strong repertoire.

Wise Publications
part of The Music Sales Group
London/New York/Paris/Sydney/Copenhagen/Berlin/Madrid/Tokyo

Published by
Wise Publications
14-15 Berners Street, London W1T 3LJ, UK.

Exclusive Distributors:
Music Sales Limited
14-15 Berners Street,
London W1T 3LJ, UK.
Music Sales Corporation
257 Park Avenue South
New York
NY10010, USA.
Music Sales Pty Limited
20 Resolution Drive,
Caringbah, NSW 2229,
Australia.

Order No. AM92381
ISBN 0-7119-4457-11
This book © Copyright 2005
Wise Publications, a division of Music Sales Limited.

Previously published as *The 6 Chord Songbook: Christmas Songs & Carols*

Music processed by The Pitts
Cover design by Chloë Alexander

Printed in the United Kingdom

Your Guarantee of Quality
As publishers, we strive to produce every book to the highest commercial standards.
The music has been freshly engraved and the book has been carefully designed to
minimise awkward page turns and to make playing from it a real pleasure.
Throughout, the printing and binding have been planned to ensure a sturdy,
attractive publication which should give years of enjoyment. If your copy fails to
meet our high standards, please inform us and we will gladly replace it.

www.musicsales.com

Relative Tuning

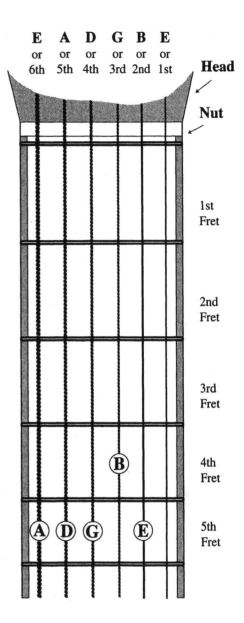

The guitar can be tuned with the aid of pitch pipes or dedicated electronic guitar tuners which are available through your local music dealer. If you do not have a tuning device, you can use relative tuning. Estimate the pitch of the 6th string as near as possible to E or at least a comfortable pitch (not too high, as you might break other strings in tuning up). Then, while checking the various positions on the diagram, place a finger from your left hand on the:

5th fret of the E or 6th string and **tune the open A** (or 5th string) to the note (A)

5th fret of the A or 5th string and **tune the open D** (or 4th string) to the note (D)

5th fret of the D or 4th string and **tune the open G** (or 3rd string) to the note (G)

4th fret of the G or 3rd string and **tune the open B** (or 2nd string) to the note (B)

5th fret of the B or 2nd string and **tune the open E** (or 1st string) to the note (E)

Reading Chord Boxes

Chord boxes are diagrams of the guitar neck viewed head upwards, face on as illustrated. The top horizontal line is the nut, unless a higher fret number is indicated, the others are the frets.

The vertical lines are the strings, starting from E (or 6th) on the left to E (or 1st) on the right.

The black dots indicate where to place your fingers.

Strings marked with an O are played open, not fretted.

Strings marked with an X should not be played.

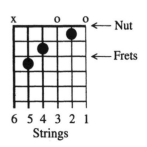

Away In A Manger

Traditional

D	G	C	Am	Em	A

Verse 1

```
D  G     D  G              C  Am
A - way in a  manger, no crib for a  bed,
          D  Em  G  A        D
The little Lord Jesus laid down His sweet head.
     G      D  Em        G          C
The stars in the bright sky looked down where He lay,
     Am D  Em   Am      D  G
The little Lord Jesus asleep on the hay.
```

Verse 2

```
D  G     D  G              C  Am
The cattle are lowing, the Baby a - wakes,
          D  Em  G  A        D
But little Lord Jesus, no crying He makes.
     G      D  Em        G          C
I love Thee, Lord Jesus, look down from the sky
     Am    D  Em     Am      D  G
And stay by my side until morning is  nigh.
```

Verse 3

```
D  G     D  G              C  Am
Be near me, Lord Jesus, I ask Thee to  stay
          D  Em  G  A        D
Close by me for ever and love me, I pray.
     G      D  Em        G          C
Bless all the dear children in Thy tender care
     Am D  Em     Am      D  G
And fit us for heaven, to live with Thee there.
```

Deck The Halls

Traditional

Verse 1

D
Deck the halls with boughs of holly
A D A D
Fa la la la la, la la la la.

'Tis the season to be jolly
A D A D
Fa la la la la, la la la la.

A   D A
Don we now our gay apparel
D E7 A E A
Fa la la, la la la, la la la.

D
Troll the ancient Yuletide Carol
G   D G D A D
Fa la la la la, la la la la.

Verse 2

D
See the blazing yule before us
A D A D
Fa la la la la, la la la la.

Strike the harp and join the chorus
A D A D
Fa la la la la, la la la la.

A   D A
Follow me in merry measur
D E7 A E A
Fa la la, la la la, la la la.

D
While I tell of Yuletide treasure
G   D G D A D
Fa la la la la, la la la la.

Good Christian Men, Rejoice

Traditional

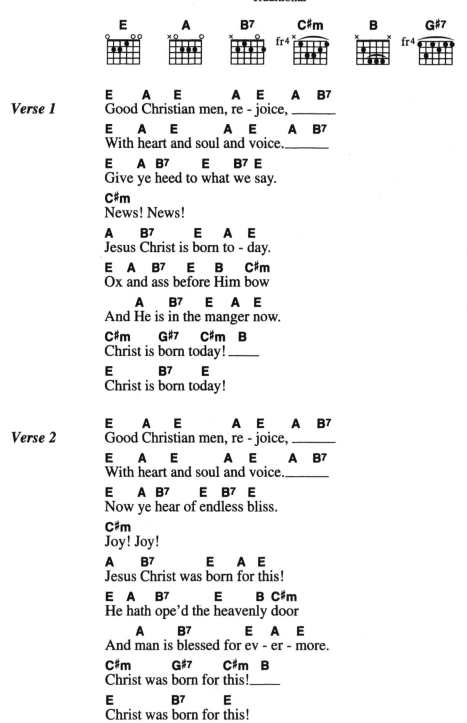

Verse 1

   E   A   E   A E   A   B7
Good Christian men, re - joice, _____

   E   A   E   A E   A   B7
With heart and soul and voice._____

   E   A B7   E   B7 E
Give ye heed to what we say.

C#m
News! News!

 A   B7   E   A   E
Jesus Christ is born to - day.

 E A B7   E   B   C#m
Ox and ass before Him bow

     A   B7   E   A   E
And He is in the manger now.

C#m   **G#7**   **C#m** **B**
Christ is born today! ____

 E   B7   E
Christ is born today!

Verse 2

   E   A   E   A E   A   B7
Good Christian men, re - joice, _____

   E   A   E   A E   A   B7
With heart and soul and voice._____

   E   A B7   E   B7 E
Now ye hear of endless bliss.

C#m
Joy! Joy!

 A   B7   E   A   E
Jesus Christ was born for this!

 E A B7   E   B C#m
He hath ope'd the heavenly door

     A   B7   E   A   E
And man is blessed for ev - er - more.

C#m   **G#7**   **C#m** **B**
Christ was born for this!____

 E   B7   E
Christ was born for this!

Verse 3

E   A   E   A   E   A   B7
Good Christian men, re - joice, _____

E   A   E   A   E   A   B7
With heart and soul and voice._____

E   A B7   E   B7 E
Now ye need not fear the grave.

C#m
Peace! Peace!

A   B7   E   A   E
Jesus Christ was born to save!

E   A B7   E   B   C#m
Calls you one and calls you all,

   A   B7 E A   E
To gain His everlasting hall.

C#m   G#7   C#m B
Christ was born to save!_____

E   B7   E
Christ was born to save!

Good King Wenceslas

Traditional

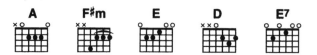

Verse 1

```
A        F#m  E   A   D    E
```
Good King Wen - ces - las looked out,

```
D   A   D    E7  A
```
On the feast of Stephen,

```
        F#m   E   A    D  E
```
When the snow lay round a - bout,

```
D    A   D    E7  A
```
Deep and crisp and even;

```
     D A   E   A    E   F#m
```
Brightly shone the moon that night,

```
D     A   D   E7  A
```
Though the frost was cruel,

```
        D   E7  F#m   E
```
When a poor man came in sight,

```
A    D    A  E  F#m D A
```
Gath'ring winter fu - el.

Verse 2

```
A       F#m E   A    D  E
```
"Hither, page and stand by me,

```
D  A   D      E7  A
```
If thou know'st it, telling.

```
      F#m E   A   D  E
```
Yonder peas-ant who is he?

```
D     A    D   E7  A
```
Where, and what his dwelling?"

```
     D A   E   A    E     F#m
```
"Sire, he lives a   good league hence,

```
D  A   D    E7  A
```
Underneath the mountain;

```
        D   E7 F#m  E
```
Right against the forest fence,

```
A   D    A  E  F#m  D A
```
By Saint Agnes fount - tain.
```
```

Verse 3

(A)　　F#m　E　A　　D　E
"Bring me flesh and bring me wine,

D　　A　D　　E7　　A
Bring me pine logs hither;

　　　　F#m　E　　A　　D　E
Thou and I　　will see him dine,

D　　A　D　　E7　　A
When we bear them hither."

　　　D　A　E　A　　E　　F#m
Page and monarch forth they went,

D　　A　D　　E7　A
Forth they went to - gether;

　　　　　D　　E7　　F#m　　E
Through the rude wind's wild lament

A　　D A E F#m　D A
And the bit-ter weath - er.

Verse 4

　　　F#m　E　A　D　E
"Sire, the night is dar-ker now,

D　　A　D　　E7　　A
And the wind blows stronger;

　　　F#m　E A　　D　E
Fails my heart, I　know not how,

D A　D　E7 A
I　can go no longer."

　　　D　A　E　　A　　E　F#m
"Mark my footsteps, good my page!

D　　A　D　E7　A
Tread thou in　them boldly:

　　　D　E7 F#m　　E
Thou shalt find the winter's rage

A　　D　A　　E　F#m D A
Freeze thy blood less cold - ly."

Verse 5

　　　F#m　E　A　　D　E
In his mas - ter's steps he trod,

D　　A　D　　E7　A
Where the snow lay dinted;

　　　F#m E A　　D E
Heat was in　the ve - ry sod

D　　A　D　E7　A
Which the saint had printed.

　　　D　A　E　A　　E　F#m
Therefore, Christian men, be　sure,

D　　A D　E7 A
Wealth or rank possessing,

　　　D　E7 F#m　　E
Ye who now will bless the poor,

A　　D　A　　E　F#m D A
Shall yourselves find bless - ing.

Hark The Herald Angels Sing

Traditional

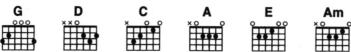

Verse 1

G   D G   D
Hark! The herald-angels sing_____

G   C   G   D G
Glory to the new born King;

              D G   A
Peace on earth, and mercy mild,

D A D   G A D
God and sinners re-con-ciled.

G   D G   D
Joyful all ye nations, rise,_____

G   D G   D
Join the triumph of the skies;_____

C   E Am E Am
With the angelic host proclaim

D   G   D G
"Christ is born in Bethle-hem!"

C   E Am E Am
Hark! The herald-an - gels sing,

D   G   D G
Glory to the new born King.

Verse 2

  (G)   **D G**   **D**
Christ by highest heaven adored, ____

G   **C**   **G D G**
Christ, the everlasting Lord;

           D G   **A**
Late in time be-hold him come,

D A   **D   G A   D**
Offspring of a Virgin's womb.

G   **D G**   **D**
Veiled in flesh the Godhead see!___

G   **D G D**
Hail the incarnate De-i-ty! ___

C   **E**   **Am E Am**
Pleased as man with man to dwell,

D   **G**   **D G**
Jesus our Emman - u - el.

C   **E** **Am E** **Am**
Hark! The herald-an - gels sing,

D   **G**   **D**   **G**
Glory to the new born King.

Verse 3

              D   **G**   **D**
Hail, the heaven born Prince of peace!___

G   **C**   **G D G**
Hail, the Son of righteousness!

            D G   **A**
Light and life to all he brings,

D   **A**   **D**   **G A**   **D**
Risen with healing in His wings,

G   **D G**   **D**
Mild he lays his glory by;___

G   **D G**   **D**
Born that man no more may die; ___

C   **E Am**   **E** **Am**
Born to raise the sons of earth;

D   **G**   **D**   **G**
Born to give them second birth.

C   **E** **Am E**   **Am**
Hark! The herald-an - gels sing,

D   **G**   **D**   **G**
Glory to the new born King.

I Saw Three Ships

Traditional

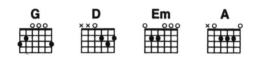

Verse 1

G   D
I saw three ships come sailing in,
  Em   A   D
On Christmas day, on Christmas day;
G   D
I saw three ships come sailing in
  G   Em   D   G
On Christmas day in the morning.

Verse 2

    G   D
And what was in those ships all three,
  Em   A   D
On Christmas day, on Christmas day;
   G   D
And what was in those ships all three,
  G   Em   D   G
On Christmas day in the morning.

Verse 3

    G   D
The Virgin Mary and Christ were there,
  Em   A   D
On Christmas day, on Christmas day;
   G   D
The Virgin Mary and Christ were there,
  G   Em   D   G
On Christmas day in the morning.

Verse 4

    G   D
Pray, whither sailed those ships all three,
  Em   A   D
On Christmas day, on Christmas day?
    G   D
Pray, whither sailed those ships all three,
  G   Em   D   G
On Christmas day in the morning?

Verse 5

```
    G              D
O they sailed into Bethlehem,
      Em           A         D
On Christmas day, on Christmas day;
    G              D
O they sailed into Bethlehem,
    G       Em      D   G
On Christmas day in the morning.
```

Verse 6

```
      G              D
And all the bells on earth shall ring,
      Em           A         D
On Christmas day, on Christmas day;
      G              D
And all the bells on earth shall ring,
    G       Em      D   G
On Christmas day in the morning.
```

Verse 7

```
      G              D
And all the angels in heaven shall sing,
      Em           A         D
On Christmas day, on Christmas day;
      G              D
And all the angels in heaven shall sing,
    G       Em      D   G
On Christmas day in the morning.
```

Verse 8

```
      G              D
And all the souls on earth shall sing,
      Em           A         D
On Christmas day, on Christmas day;
      G              D
And all the souls on earth shall sing,
    G       Em      D   G
On Christmas day in the morning.
```

Verse 9

```
      G         D
Then let us all rejoice again,
      Em           A         D
On Christmas day, on Christmas day;
      G         D
Then let us all rejoice again,
    G       Em      D   G
On Christmas day in the morning.
```

In The Bleak Midwinter

Traditional

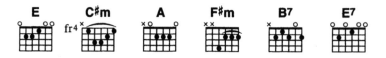

Verse 1

E   C#m
In the bleak midwinter

A   F#m B7
Frosty wind made moan, ___

E   C#m
Earth stood hard as iron,

A   B7   E
Water like a stone.

A   E7 A   C#m
Snow had fallen, snow on snow,

E   A B7
Snow on snow.

E   C#m
In the bleak midwinter,

A   B7   E
Long___ ago.

Verse 2

                  C#m
Our God, heaven cannot hold Him

A   F#m B7
Nor earth sustain; ___

E   C#m
Heaven and earth shall flee away

A   B7   E
When He comes to reign:

A   E7 A C#m
In the bleak midwinter

   E   A   B7
A stable place sufficed

      E   C#m
The Lord God Almighty

A B7 E
Je-sus Christ.

Verse 3

       (E)   C#m
Enough for Him, whom Cherubim

A   F#m B7
Worship night and day, ___

     E   C#m
A breastful of milk

      A   B7   E
And a mangerful of hay;

    A   E7   A   C#m
Enough for Him, whom An - gels

E A   B7
Fall down before,

     E   C#m
The ox and ass and camel

A   B7 E
Which a - dore.

Verse 4

               C#m
Angels and Archangels

A   F#m B7
May have gathered there, ___

E   C#m
Cherubim and Seraphim

A   B7   E
Throngèd the air:

    A   E7 A C#m
But only his mother

E   A   B7
In her maiden bliss

E   C#m
Worshipped the belovèd

A   B7 E
With a   kiss.

Verse 5

              C#m
What can I give Him,

A   F#m B7
Poor as I am? ___

E   C#m
If I were a shepherd

A   B7   E
I would bring a lamb;

A   E7 A   C#m
If I were a wise man

E   A   B7
I would do my part;

     E   C#m
Yet what can I give Him

A   B7 E
Give my heart.

15

Jingle Bells

Traditional

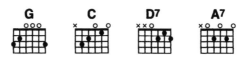

Verse 1

G
Dashing through the snow
C
In a one-horse open sleigh,
D7
O'er the fields we go,
G
Laughing all the way.

Bells on bobtail ring
C
Making spirits bright.
G
What fun it is to ride and sing
D7   **G**
A sleighing song tonight.

Chorus 1

(G)
Jingle bells, jingle bells,

Jingle all the way.
C   **D7**   **C G**
Oh, what fun it is to ride
  A7   **D7**
In a one-horse open sleigh.
  G
Oh, jingle bells, jingle bells,

Jingle all the way.
C   **G**
Oh, what fun it is to ride
  D7   **G**
In a one-horse open sleigh.

Verse 2

(G)
Now the ground is white,
             C
Go it while you're young,
           D7
Take the girls tonight,
             G
Sing this sleighing song.

Get a bobtailed bay,
            C
Two-forty for his speed,
             G
Then hitch him to an open sleigh
D7   **G**
And you will take the lead.

Chorus 2

(G)
Jingle bells, jingle bells,

Jingle all the way.
C   **D7**   **C G**
Oh, what fun it is to ride
    A7   **D7**
In a one-horse open sleigh.
    G
Oh, jingle bells, jingle bells,

Jingle all the way.
C   **G**
Oh, what fun it is to ride
   D7   **G**
In a one-horse open sleigh.

O Christmas Tree

Traditional

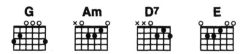

G
O Christmas Tree,

O Christmas Tree,
    Am   D7   G
You stand in verdant beauty!

O Christmas Tree,

O Christmas Tree,
    Am   D7   G
You stand in verdant beauty!
                   E   Am
Your boughs are green in summer's glow
    D7   G
And do not fade in winter's snow.

O Christmas Tree,

O Christmas Tree,
    Am   D7   G
You stand in verdant beauty!

Original German Words:

O Tannenbaum,
O Tannenbaum,
Vie treu sind deine blätter.
O Tannenbaum,
O Tannenbaum,
Vie treu sind deine blätter.
Du grünst nicht nur zur sommerzeit nein,
Auch im winter wenn es schneit.
O Tannenbaum,
O Tannenbaum,
Vie treu sind deine blätter.

Silent Night

Traditional

Verse 1

C
Silent night, holy night!

G7   C
All is calm, all is bright.

F   C
Round yon Virgin mother and child,

F   C
Holy infant so tender and mild.

G7   C
Sleep in heavenly peace,___

        G7   C
Sleep in heavenly peace.

Verse 2

C
Silent night, holy night,

G7   C
Shepherds wake at the sight;

F   C
Glory streams from heaven afar,

F   C
Heaven hosts sing Alleluia.

G7   C
Christ the Saviour is born!___

        G7   C
Christ the Saviour is born!

Verse 3

C
Silent night, holy night,

G7   C
Son of God, love's pure light;

F   C
Radiance beams from Thy holy face,

F   C
With the dawn of redeeming grace,

G7   C
Jesus, Lord at Thy birth, ___

        G7   C
Jesus, Lord at Thy birth.

O Come All Ye Faithful

Traditional

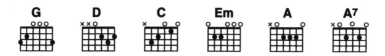

Verse 1

G   D
O come, all ye faithful,

G D G C G D
Joy-ful and tri-umphant.

Em D A D G D G D A⁷ D
O come ye, o come___ye to Beth - lehem.

G D G D G
Come and be-hold Him,

D G Em C D
Born the King of Angels.

G   D G D G
O come, let us a - dore Him,

      D G D G   D
O come, let us a - dore Him,

G D   G D A D G C
O come, let us a - dore Him,___

G   D G
Christ___the Lord.

Verse 2

      D
God of God,

G D G C G D
Light___of___light,___

Em D A D G D G D A⁷ D
Lo! He ab-hors___not the Vir - gin's womb;

G D G D G
Ver - y God,___

  D G Em C D
Begot-ten, not cre-ated:

G   D G D G
O come, let us a - dore Him,

      D G D G   D
O come, let us a - dore Him,

G D   G D A D G C
O come, let us a - dore Him,___

G   D G
Christ___the Lord.

Verse 3

(G)   D
Sing Choirs of Angels,

G   D G   C   G   D
Sing in ex - ul - ta - tion,

Em   D   A   D   G D   G D   A7   D
Sing all ye cit - i - zens of heaven above;

G   D   G   D   G
Glo-ry to God ___

D   G   Em C   D
In ___ the ___ highest:

G   D G D   G
O come, let us a - dore Him,

            D G D   G   D
O come, let us a - dore Him,

G   D   G D A D   G   C
O   come, let us a - dore Him, ___

G   D   G
Christ ___ the Lord.

Verse 4

                D
Yea, Lord, we greet Thee,

G   D   G C G   D
Born this happy morning,

Em D   A   D   G D   G   D   A7 D
Je - su, to thee ___ be ___ glo - ry given;

G   D G   D G
Word of the Father,

D   G Em   C   D
Now in flesh ap-pearing:

G   D G D   G
O come, let us a - dore Him,

          D G D   G   D
O come, let us a - dore Him,

G   D   G D A D   G   C
O   come, let us a - dore Him, ___

G   D   G
Christ ___ the Lord.

O Come, O Come, Emmanuel

Traditional

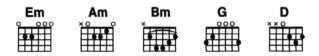

Em   Am Em

Verse 1   O come, o come, Emmanuel,

                        Am Bm   Em

And ransom captive Is - ra - el,

Am   G   D

That mourns in lonely exile here,

Em D   G   Am D   G

Un - til the Son of God ___ appear.

D   G   Bm Em

Re - joice! Re - joice!

Bm Am D   Em

Em - ma - nu-el

D   G   Em

Shall come to thee

   Am Bm   Em

O Is - ra - el!

                                Am   Em

Verse 2   O come, Thou dayspring, come and cheer

                     Am Bm Em

Our spirits by Thine ad - vent here:

Am   G   D

Disperse the gloomy clouds of night

Em D   G   Am D G

And death's dark shadows put ___ to flight.

D   G   Bm Em

Re - joice! Re - joice!

Bm Am D   Em

Em - ma - nu-el

D   G   Em

Shall come to thee

   Am Bm   Em

O Is - ra - el!

Verse 3

(Em)   **Am**   **Em**
O come, Thou wisdom from on high

           Am Bm Em
And order all things, far and nigh:

Am   **G**   **D**
To us the path of knowledge show

Em D   **G**   **Am**   **D** **G**
And cause us in her ways ___ to go.

D   **G**   **Bm Em**
Re - joice! Re - joice!

Bm Am D   **Em**
Em - ma - nu-el

D   **G**   **Em**
Shall come to thee

   Am Bm   **Em**
O Is - ra - el!

Verse 4

          Am   **Em**
O come, desire of nations, bind

          Am **Bm** **Em**
All peoples in one heart ___ and mind;

Am   **G**   **D**
Bid envy, strife, and quarrels cease;

Em D   **G**   **Am D**   **G**
Fill the whole world with hea - ven's peace.

D   **G**   **Bm Em**
Re - joice! Re - joice!

Bm Am D   **Em**
Em - ma - nu-el

D   **G**   **Em**
Shall come to thee

   Am Bm   **Em**
O Is - ra - el!

O Little Town Of Bethlehem

Traditional

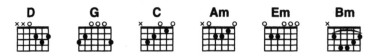

Verse 1

D   G C G   Am G   Em D
O lit-tle town of Beth - le - hem,

Em Am G C   D   G
How still we see thee lie!

D   G   C G   Am G   Em D
A - bove thy deep and dreamless sleep

Em Am G   C   D G
The si - lent stars go by.

Em Bm   C   D   G Em D
Yet in the dark streets shi - neth

G   Am Em D
The ever-last - ing light:

Em D G   C G   Am G Em D
The ___ hopes and fears of   all the years

Em Am G C   D G
Are met in Thee to-night.

Verse 2

D G   C G   Am G Em D
O morning stars, to - geth - er,

Em Am   G C D G
Pro - claim the Ho-ly birth,

D   G   C G   Am G   Em D
And praises sing to   God the King,

Em Am   G C   D   G
And peace to men on earth;

Em Bm   C   D G Em D
For Christ is born of Ma - ry,

G   Am Em D
And gathered all   a - bove,

Em   D   G   C G   Am G Em D
While___ mortals sleep the Angels keep

Em Am   G C   D   G
Their watch of wondering love.

Verse 3

D   G C   G Am G Em D
How si - lent - ly, how si - lent - ly,

Em Am G   C D G
The wondrous gift is given!

D G   C G   Am G Em D
So God im-parts to   hu-man hearts

Em Am G C D G
The blessing of His heaven.

Em Bm   C   D G Em D
No ear may hear His com - ing;

    G   Am   Em D
But in this world of   sin,

Em   D G   C   G Am G   Em D
Where ___ meek souls will re - ceive Him, still

Em Am G   C D G
The dear Christ en-ters in.

Verse 4

D   G C   G   Am G Em D
Where children pure and hap - py

Em Am G C   D G
Pray to   the blessèd Child,

D   G   C G Am G Em D
Where mis - er - y cries out to   Thee,

Em Am G C D G
Son of   the mother mild;

Em   Bm C D   G   Em D
Where charity stands watch - ing

    G   Am   Em D
And faith holds wide the   door,

Em D G   C   G   Am G   Em D
The ___ dark night wakes, the glo - ry   breaks,

Em Am G   C   D   G
And Christmas comes once more.

Verse 5

D G C G   Am G   Em D
O ho - ly Child of   Beth - le - hem,

Em Am G C D G
Des-cend to us we pray;

D   G   C G Am G Em D
Cast out our sin and en-ter in,

Em Am G C D G
Be born in us to-day.

Em Bm   C   D G Em D
We hear the Christmas An - gels

    G   Am Em D
The great glad tid - ings tell:

Em D G   C G Am G   Em D
O___ come to us, a - bide with us,

Em Am G C   D G
Our Lord Emman - u - el.

Once In Royal David's City

Traditional

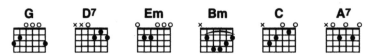

G   D7   Em   Bm   C   A7

Verse 1

G   D7 G   D7   G
Once in   Royal David's city

      Em Bm   C D7 G
Stood a   lowly cat-tle shed.

           D7 G   A7   D7 G
Where a mother laid her ba - by,

    Em Bm   C D7 G
In a   manger for His bed.

C   G   D7   G
Mary was that mother mild,

C   G   C D7 G
Jesus Christ her lit-tle Child.

Verse 2

       D7   G   D7   G
He came down to earth from heaven

      Em Bm   C   D7 G
Who is   God and Lord of all,

       D7 G   A7   D7 G
And His shelter was a sta-ble,

      Em Bm   C D7 G
And His cradle was a   stall.

C   G   D7   G
With the poor and mean and lowly

C   G   C D7   G
Lived on earth our Sa-viour holy.

Verse 3

       D7   G   D7   G
And through all His wondrous childhood

    Em   Bm   C D7 G
He would honour and ob - ey,

       D7 G   A7   D7 G
Love and watch the lowly maiden,

     Em   Bm   C   D7 G
In whose gentle arms He lay.

C   G   D7   G
Christian children all must be,

C   G   C   D7 G
Mild, obedient, good as He.

Verse 4

(G) D7 G   D7   G
For He   is our childhood's pattern,

      Em Bm C   D7   G
Day by   day like us He grew,

      D7 G   A7   D7 G
He was little, weak and helpless,

        Em Bm   C   D7   G
Tears and smiles like us He knew,

C   G   D7   G
And He feeleth for our sadness,

C   G   C D7 G
And He shareth in our gladness.

Verse 5

        D7 G   D7   G
And our eyes at last shall see Him,

          Em Bm   C   D7 G
Through His own redeeming love,

        D7 G   A7   D7 G
For that child so dear and gen-tle

    Em Bm   C D7   G
Is our Lord in heaven above,

C   G   D7   G
And He leads his children on

C   G   C D7 G
To the place where He is   gone.

Verse 6

        D7 G   D7   G
Not in   that poor lowly stable,

      Em Bm C   D7   G
With the   oxen standing by,

      D7 G   A7   D7 G
We shall see Him, but in heaven

      Em Bm   C   D7 G
Set at   God's right hand on high,

C   G   D7   G
Where, like stars, His children crowned

C   G   C   D7 G
All in white shall wait a - round.

Sussex Carol

Traditional

G   C   D Am^6 $Cmaj^7$ D^7

Verse 1

     G   C   G   D
On Christmas night all Christians sing,
       G   C   G D G
To hear the news the An-gels bring.
             C   G   D
On Christmas night all Christians sing,
       G   C   G D G
To hear the news the Angels bring.
D Am^6 G $Cmaj^7$ D   Am
News of great joy, news of great   mirth, ____
G   C D C D^7 G
News of our merciful King's birth.

Verse 2

            C   G   D
Then why should men on earth be so sad,
       G   C   G   D G
Since our Redeemer made us glad.
            C   G   D
Then why should men on earth be so sad,
       G   C   G   D G
Since our Redeemer made us glad.
D Am^6 G $Cmaj^7$ D   Am
When from our sin He set us   free, ____
G   C D C D^7 G
All for to gain our liberty.

Verse 3

      (G)   C   G   D
When sin departs before His grace,

        G   C   G D G
Then life and health come in its place;

           C   G   D
When sin departs before His grace,

        G   C   G D G
Then life and health come in its place;

D Am^6 G $Cmaj^7$ D   Am
An-gels and men with joy may   sing,____

G   C D C D^7 G
All for to see the new-born King.

Verse 4

           C   G   D
All out of darkness we have light,

        G   C   G D G
Which made the Angels sing this night;

           C   G   D
All out of darkness we have light,

        G   C   G D G
Which made the Angels sing this night;

D Am^6 G $Cmaj^7$ D   Am
"Glory to God and peace to   men, ____

G   C D C D^7 G
Now and for evermore. Amen."

The First Nowell

Traditional

D	Bm	A	A7	G	F#m

Verse 1

D   Bm A A7 D   G D
The first No - well the Angels did say,

A7   D   A7 D G   A7 D   A7 D
Was to certain poor shepherds in fields as they lay;

A7 D   Bm   A   A7 D   G   D
In fields where they lay keeping their sheep,

A7 D   G   D G A7 D A7 D
On a cold winter's night __ that was so deep.

A7 D   G   F#m D G   D   A
No-well, No-well, No-well, No-well, __

Bm   G D   G A D A7 D
Born is the King __ of Is - ra - el.

Verse 2

Bm A A7 D G D
They lookèd up and saw a star,

A7   D A7 D   G A7 D   A7   D
Shining in the East, __ be - yond them far,

A7 D Bm A   A7 D   G   D
And to the   earth it gave great light,

A7 D   G   D G A7   D   A7 D
And so it con-tin-ued both day and night.

A7 D   G   F#m D G   D   A
No-well, No-well, No-well, No-well, __

Bm   G D   G A D A7 D
Born is the King __ of Is - ra - el.

Verse 3

Bm A   A7 D G   D
And by the light of that same Star,

A7   D   A7 D   G A7   D   A7 D
Three Wisemen came __ from country far;

A7 D Bm A   A7 D G D
To seek for a King was their in - tent,

A7   D   G D G A7   D   A7 D
And to follow the Star __ wherever it went.

A7 D   G   F#m D G   D   A
No-well, No-well, No-well, No-well, __

Bm   G D   G A D A7 D
Born is the King __ of Is - ra - el.

Verse 4

(D)   Bm A A7 D   G   D
This Star drew nigh un - to the north-west,

A7 D   A7 D G A7 D   A7 D
O'er Beth - le - hem ___ it took its rest,

A7 D   Bm A A7 D   G   D
And there it   did both stop and stay

A7   D   G   D   G A7   D A7 D
Right over the place ___ where Je-sus lay.

A7 D   G F#m D G   D   A
No-well, No-well, No-well, No-well, ___

Bm   G D   G A D A7 D
Born is the King ___ of Is - ra - el.

Verse 5

          Bm A A7   D   G   D
Then entered in those Wisemen three,

A7 D A7   D G A7 D A7   D
Full rev'rent - ly ___ up - on their knee,

A7 D   Bm A   A7 D G D
And of - fered there, in His presence,

A7   D   G   D   G A7 D   A7 D
Their gold and myrrh ___ and frankin - cense.

A7 D   G F#m D G   D   A
No-well, No-well, No-well, No-well, ___

Bm   G D   G A D A7 D
Born is the King ___ of Is - ra - el.

Verse 6

          Bm A A7 D   G   D
Then let us   all with one ac - cord,

A7 D A7 D G A7 D   A7 D
Sing praises to ___ our Heavenly Lord,

A7 D   Bm A   A7 D   G D
That hath made Heaven and earth of nought,

A7 D   G   D   G A7 D   A7 D
And with His blood ___ mankind hath bought.

A7 D   G F#m D G   D   A
No-well, No-well, No-well, No-well, ___

Bm   G D   G A D A7 D
Born is the King ___ of Is - ra - el.

The Holly And The Ivy

Traditional

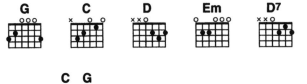

Verse 1

```
G              C  G
The holly and the ivy,
                 C   G
When they are both full grown,
D  Em              C      D
Of all the trees that are in the wood,
    G     C    D7 G
The holly wears the crown.
C   G      C  G                         C  D
The rising of the sun and the running of the deer,
      Em        G  C    D           G     C D7 G
The playing of the merry organ, sweet singing in the choir.
```

Verse 2

```
                 C  G
The holly bears a  blossom,
                 C  G
As white as the lily flower,
D   Em            C    D
And Mary bore sweet Jesus Christ,
    G     C    D7 G
To be our sweet Saviour.
C   G      C  G                         C  D
The rising of the sun and the running of the deer,
      Em        G  C    D           G     C D7 G
The playing of the merry organ, sweet singing in the choir.
```

Verse 3

```
G               C  G
The holly bears a  berry,
         C  G
As red as any blood,
D   Em            C    D
And Mary bore sweet Jesus Christ
    G     C D7  G
To do poor sin-ners good.
C   G      C  G                         C  D
The rising of the sun and the running of the deer,
      Em        G  C    D           G     C D7 G
The playing of the merry organ, sweet singing in the choir.
```

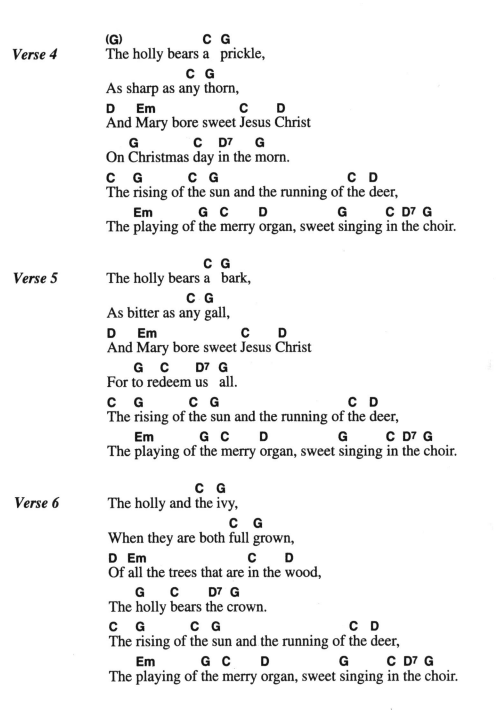

Verse 4

   (G)   **C G**
The holly bears a prickle,

           C G
As sharp as any thorn,

D Em   **C   D**
And Mary bore sweet Jesus Christ

   G   **C D⁷** **G**
On Christmas day in the morn.

C G   **C G**   **C D**
The rising of the sun and the running of the deer,

    Em   **G C**   **D**   **G**   **C D⁷ G**
The playing of the merry organ, sweet singing in the choir.

Verse 5

           C G
The holly bears a bark,

           C G
As bitter as any gall,

D Em   **C   D**
And Mary bore sweet Jesus Christ

   G C   **D⁷ G**
For to redeem us all.

C G   **C G**   **C D**
The rising of the sun and the running of the deer,

    Em   **G C**   **D**   **G**   **C D⁷ G**
The playing of the merry organ, sweet singing in the choir.

Verse 6

           C G
The holly and the ivy,

           C G
When they are both full grown,

D Em   **C   D**
Of all the trees that are in the wood,

   G   **C**   **D⁷ G**
The holly bears the crown.

C G   **C G**   **C D**
The rising of the sun and the running of the deer,

    Em   **G C**   **D**   **G**   **C D⁷ G**
The playing of the merry organ, sweet singing in the choir.

The Mistletoe Bough

Traditional

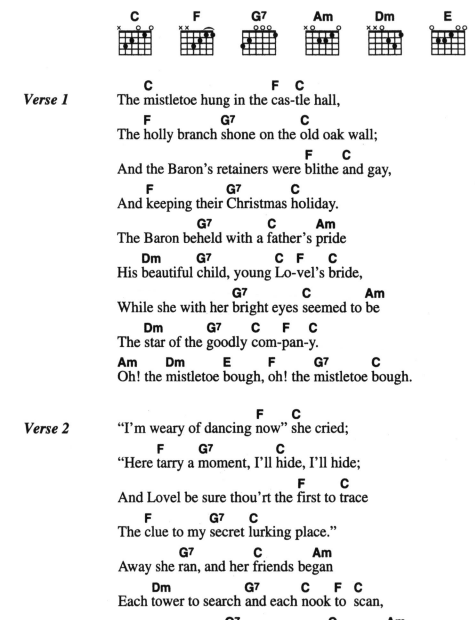

Verse 1

    C   F C
The mistletoe hung in the cas-tle hall,
    F   G7   C
The holly branch shone on the old oak wall;
                          F   C
And the Baron's retainers were blithe and gay,
    F   G7   C
And keeping their Christmas holiday.
        G7   C   Am
The Baron beheld with a father's pride
    Dm   G7   C F   C
His beautiful child, young Lo-vel's bride,
                  G7   C   Am
While she with her bright eyes seemed to be
    Dm   G7   C F   C
The star of the goodly com-pan-y.
Am   Dm   E   F   G7   C
Oh! the mistletoe bough, oh! the mistletoe bough.

Verse 2

                      F   C
"I'm weary of dancing now" she cried;
     F   G7   C
"Here tarry a moment, I'll hide, I'll hide;
                         F   C
And Lovel be sure thou'rt the first to trace
    F   G7   C
The clue to my secret lurking place."
      G7   C   Am
Away she ran, and her friends began
    Dm   G7   C F C
Each tower to search and each nook to scan,
            G7   C   Am
And young Lovel cried "Oh where dost thou hide!
    Dm   G7   C F   C
I'm lonesome without thee my own dear bride."
Am   Dm   E   F   G7   C
Oh! the mistletoe bough, oh! the mistletoe bough.

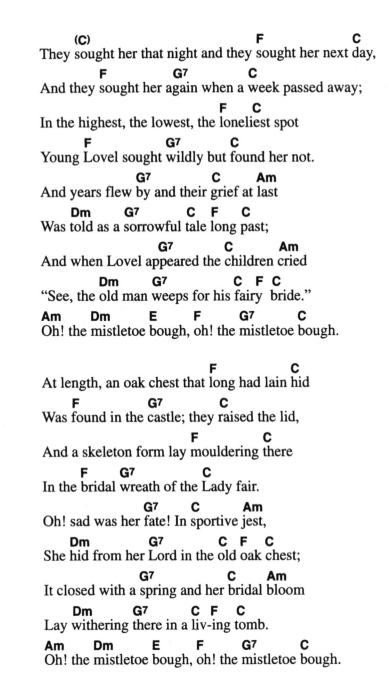

Verse 3

       (C)   **F**   **C**
They sought her that night and they sought her next day,

      F   **G7**   **C**
And they sought her again when a week passed away;

            F **C**
In the highest, the lowest, the loneliest spot

      F   **G7**   **C**
Young Lovel sought wildly but found her not.

         G7   **C** **Am**
And years flew by and their grief at last

     Dm **G7**   **C** **F** **C**
Was told as a sorrowful tale long past;

          G7   **C** **Am**
And when Lovel appeared the children cried

      Dm **G7**   **C** **F C**
"See, the old man weeps for his fairy bride."

Am **Dm**   **E** **F**   **G7**   **C**
Oh! the mistletoe bough, oh! the mistletoe bough.

Verse 4

             F   **C**
At length, an oak chest that long had lain hid

  F   **G7**   **C**
Was found in the castle; they raised the lid,

            F   **C**
And a skeleton form lay mouldering there

  F **G7**   **C**
In the bridal wreath of the Lady fair.

        G7 **C**   **Am**
Oh! sad was her fate! In sportive jest,

    Dm   **G7**   **C** **F** **C**
She hid from her Lord in the old oak chest;

        G7   **C** **Am**
It closed with a spring and her bridal bloom

    Dm   **G7**   **C** **F** **C**
Lay withering there in a liv-ing tomb.

Am   **Dm**   **E**   **F**   **G7**   **C**
Oh! the mistletoe bough, oh! the mistletoe bough.

Unto Us A Boy Is Born

Traditional

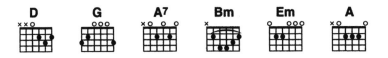

Verse 1

D   G A⁷   D
Unto us a boy is born!

      G A⁷   G D
King of all cre - a - tion,

Bm Em A D Em   A
Came He to a world forlorn,

Bm D   A⁷ | Bm G | A A⁷ | D
The Lord of every na - - - - - tion.

Verse 2

         G A⁷   D
Cradled in a stall was He

      G   A⁷ G D
With sleepy cows and as - ses;

Bm Em A D Em   A
But the ve - ry beasts could see

Bm D   A⁷ | Bm G | A A⁷ | D
That He all men sur-pas - - - - - ses.

Verse 3

        G   A⁷   D
Herod than with fear was filled:

          G   A⁷ G D
"A prince," he said, "in Jewry!"

Bm Em A D Em A
All the lit-tle boys he killed

Bm D   A⁷ | Bm G | A A⁷ | D
At Bethlehem in his fu - - - - - ry.

Verse 4

(D)   **G A⁷**   **D**
Now may Mary's Son, who came

        G A⁷ G   D
So long ago to   love us,

Bm Em A D   Em   A
Lead us   all with hearts aflame

Bm D   **A⁷ | Bm   G | A A⁷ | D**
Un - to the joys a - bo - - - - - ve us.

Verse 5

        G A⁷   **D**
Omega and Alpha He!

        G A⁷ G   D
Let the or-gan thunder,

Bm   Em A   D   Em   A
While the choir with peals of glee,

Bm D   **A⁷ | Bm   G | A A⁷ | D**
Doth rend the air a - sun - - - - - der.

We Three Kings Of Orient Are

Traditional

Em   B7   D   G   Am   C

Verse 1

Em   B7   Em
We three kings of Orient are,

                    B7   Em
Bearing gifts we traverse afar,

                D   G
Field and fountain, moor and mountain,

Am   Em B7 Em
Following yon-der star.

D   G   C   G
O_ star of wonder, star of night,

              C   G
Star with royal beauty bright.

              D   C   D
Westward leading, still proceeding,

G   C   G
Guide us to the perfect light.

Verse 2

Em   B7   Em
Born a King on Bethlehem's plain,

                    B7   Em
Gold I bring, to crown Him again,

                D   G
King for ever, ceasing never,

Am   Em B7 Em
Over us all to reign.

D   G   C   G
O_ star of wonder, star of night,

              C   G
Star with royal beauty bright.

              D   C   D
Westward leading, still proceeding,

G   C   G
Guide us to the perfect light.

Verse 3

```
Em              B7        Em
Frankincense to offer have I,
                 B7        Em
God on earth yet Priest on high
            D       G
Prayer and praising, all men raising
Am           Em B7  Em
Worshipping God most high.
D   G           C    G
O__ star of wonder, star of night,
                C      G
Star with royal beauty bright.
            D     C     D
Westward leading, still proceeding,
G             C    G
Guide us to the perfect light.
```

Verse 4

```
Em              B7        Em
Myrrh is mine, its bitter perfume
                 B7        Em
Breathes a life of gathering gloom;
            D       G
Sorrowing, sighing, bleeding, dying,
Am           Em B7  Em
Sealed in the stone-cold tomb.
D   G           C    G
O__ star of wonder, star of night,
                C      G
Star with royal beauty bright.
            D     C     D
Westward leading, still proceeding,
G             C    G
Guide us to the perfect light.
```

Verse 5

```
Em              B7        Em
Glorious now behold Him arise,
                 B7   Em
King and God and sacrifice,
        D   G
Alleluia, Alleluia;
Am           Em B7   Em
Earth to the hea-vens replies.
D   G           C    G
O__ star of wonder, star of night,
                C      G
Star with royal beauty bright.
            D     C     D
Westward leading, still proceeding,
G             C    G
Guide us to the perfect light.
```

We Wish You A Merry Christmas

Traditional

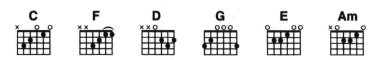

Verse 1

   C   F
We wish you a merry Christmas,

    D   G
We wish you a merry Christmas,

   C   E   Am
We wish you a merry Christmas

C F   G C
And a happy New Year.

Chorus 1

G   C   D G
Good tidings we bring

E Am   D   G
To you and your kin;

   C   G   D   G
We wish you a merry Christmas

C F   G C
And a happy New Year.

Verse 2

    C   F
Now bring us some figgy pudding,

    D   G
Now bring us some figgy pudding,

    C   E   Am
Now bring us some figgy pudding

C F   G C
And bring some out here.

Chorus 2

G   C   D G
Good tidings we bring

E Am   D   G
To you and your kin;

   C   G   D   G
We wish you a merry Christmas

C F   G   C
And a happy New Year.

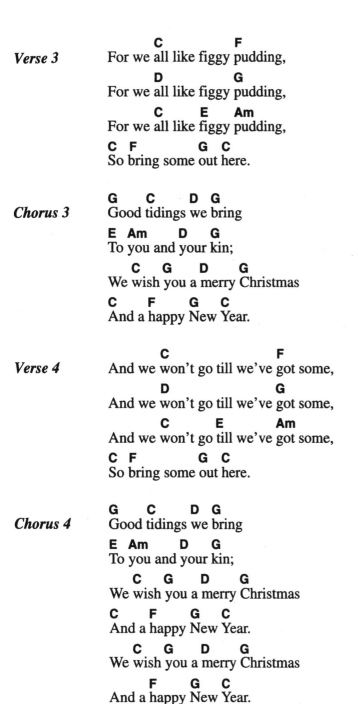

Verse 3

       C   F
For we all like figgy pudding,
        D   G
For we all like figgy pudding,
       C   E   Am
For we all like figgy pudding,
C F   G C
So bring some out here.

Chorus 3

G   C   D G
Good tidings we bring
E Am   D   G
To you and your kin;
    C   G   D   G
We wish you a merry Christmas
C   F   G   C
And a happy New Year.

Verse 4

         C   F
And we won't go till we've got some,
         D   G
And we won't go till we've got some,
        C   E   Am
And we won't go till we've got some,
C F   G C
So bring some out here.

Chorus 4

G   C   D G
Good tidings we bring
E Am   D   G
To you and your kin;
    C   G   D   G
We wish you a merry Christmas
C   F   G   C
And a happy New Year.
    C   G   D   G
We wish you a merry Christmas
      F   G   C
And a happy New Year.

What Child Is This
(Greensleeves)

Traditional

Verse 1

    Em D G   D
What Child is this, who, laid to rest,

   Em   C   B
On Mary's lap is sleeping?

    Em D G   D
Whom An - gels greet with anthems sweet,

    Em   B   Em
While shepherds watch are keeping?

Refrain

G   D
This, this is Christ the King,

    Em   C   B
Whom shepherds guard and Angels sing.

G   D
Haste, haste to bring Him laud,

   Em   B   Em
The Babe, the Son of Mary.

Verse 2

     D G   D
Why lies He in such mean estate

    Em   C   B
Where ox and ass are feeding?

    Em D G   D
Good Christian, fear for sinners here

   Em B   Em
The silent Word is pleading.

Refrain

G   D
This, this is Christ the King,

    Em   C   B
Whom shepherds guard and Angels sing.

G   D
Haste, haste to bring Him laud,

   Em   B   Em
The Babe, the Son of Mary.

Verse 3

(Em) D   G   D
So bring Him incense, gold and myrrh

     Em   C   B
Come peasant, king, to own Him;

     Em D G   D
The King of Kings salvation brings

     Em   B   Em
Let loving hearts enthrone Him.

Refrain

G   D
This, this is Christ the King,

     Em   C   B
Whom shepherds guard and Angels sing.

G   D
Haste, haste to bring Him laud,

     Em   B   Em
The Babe, the Son of Mary.

While Shepherds Watched Their Flocks By Night

Traditional

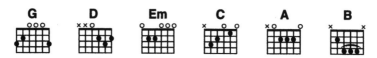

Verse 1

G   D   Em C   G
While shepherds watched their flocks by night,

D G   A D
All seated on the ground,

G   C G C G D·   Em   B
The Angel of the Lord came down,

G   D   Em C   D G
And glo-ry   shone a - round.

Verse 2

D   Em C   G
"Fear not," said he; for   mighty dread

D   G   A   D
Had seized their troubled mind;

G   C G   C ·G   D   Em B
"Glad tid-ings of great joy I   bring

G D   Em C D   G
To you and   all mankind."

Verse 3

D   Em C   G
"To you in David's   town this day

D G   A   D
Is   born of David's line

G C G   C   G D   Em B
A Saviour, who is   Christ the   Lord;

G   D   Em C D G
And this shall be the sign:

Verse 4

D   Em C   G
The heavenly Babe you there shall find

D G   A D
To human view displayed,

G   C   G C   G D   Em B
All meanly   wrapped in   swathing   bands

G   D   Em C   D   G
And in a   manger laid."

Verse 5

  (G)   **D Em C**   **G**
Thus spake the Seraph; and forthwith

D G   **A D**
Ap-peared a shining throng

G C G C G D   Em   B
Of Angels praising God, who thus

G D   Em C D G
Ad-dressed their joy-ful song:

Verse 6

             D Em C   **G**
"All glory be to God on high,

D G   **A D**
And to the earth be peace;

G   C G   C   G   D   Em B
Good-will henceforth from heaven to men

G D Em C D G
Be-gin and ne-ver cease."

The Twelve Days Of Christmas

Traditional

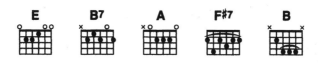

Verse 1

        E   **B7**   **E**
On the first day of Christmas my true love sent to me
  A   **E** **B7** **E**
A partridge in a pear tree.

Verse 2

        E   **B7**   **E**
On the second day of Christmas my true love sent to me
B7   **E** **A**   **E** **B7** **E**
Two turtle doves and a partridge in a pear tree.

Verse 3

        E   **B7**   **E**
On the third day of Christmas my true love sent to me

Three French hens,

Two turtle doves

      A   **E** **B7** **E**
And a partridge in a pear tree.

Verse 4

        E   **B7**   **E**
On the fourth day of Christmas my true love sent to me
B7
Four colly birds,

Three French hens, two turtle doves

      E **A**   **E** **B7** **E**
And a partridge in a pear tree.

Verse 5

        E   **B7**   **E**
On the fifth day of Christmas my true love sent to me
   F#7 **B**
Five gold rings,
E   **A**   **B7**
Four colly birds, three French hens, two turtle doves
      E **A**   **E** **B7** **E**
And a partridge in a pear tree.

Verse 6

    E   **B7**   **E**
On the sixth day of Christmas my true love sent to me
B7
Six geese a-laying,
E   **F#7** **B**
Five gold rings,
E   **A**   **B7**
Four colly birds, three French hens, two turtle doves
        E **A**   **E** **B7** **E**
And a partridge in a pear tree.

Verse 7

    E   **B7**   **E**
On the seventh day of Christmas my true love sent to me
B7
Seven swans a-swimming,

Six geese a-laying,
E   **F#7** **B**
Five gold rings, *etc.*

Verse 8

    E   **B7**   **E**
On the eighth day of Christmas my true love sent to me
B7
Eight maids a-milking,

Seven swans a-swimming, six geese a-laying,
E   **F#7** **B**
Five gold rings, *etc*

Verse 9

    E   **B7**   **E**
On the ninth day of Christmas my true love sent to me
B7
Nine drummers drumming,

Eight maids a-milking, seven swans a-swimming, six geese a-laying,
E   **F#7** **B**
Five gold rings, *etc*

Verse 10

    E   **B7**   **E**
On the tenth day of Christmas my true love sent to me
B7
Ten pipers piping,

Nine drummers drumming, Eight maids a-milking,

Seven swans a-swimming, six geese a-laying,
E   **F#7** **B**
Five gold rings, *etc*

Verse 11

     E   **B7**   **E**
On the eleventh day of Christmas my true love sent to me

B7
Eleven Ladies dancing,

Ten pipers piping, nine drummers drumming, eight maids a-milking,

Seven swans a-swimming, six geese a-laying,

E **F#7** **B**
Five gold rings, *etc*

Verse 12

     E   **B7**   **E**
On the twelth day of Christmas my true love sent to me

B7
Twelve Lords a-leaping,

Eleven Ladies dancing,

Ten pipers piping,

Nine drummers drumming,

Eight maids a-milking,

Seven swans a-swimming,

Six geese a-laying,

E **F#7** **B**
Five gold rings,

E
Four colly birds,

A
Three French hens,

B7
Two turtle doves

     E **A** **E** **B7** **E**
And a partridge in a pear tree.